LOVE THE LOVELESS
for kids

A STUDY ON JONAH

LOVEGODGREATLY.COM

A Word to Parents

This book grew out of a desire to provide a companion study journal for children to use alongside the *Love the Loveless: A study on Jonah* adult study journal and book.

Love God Greatly is dedicated to making God's Word available to our beautiful community of women… and now, women have the opportunity to share God's Word with children through this study uniquely crafted for young hearts.

CONTENTS

INTRODUCTION

LOVE THE LOVELESS

If you have already heard the story of Jonah being swallowed by a great fish and then rescued by God, you might think it sounds like a movie. Perhaps you are wondering how a man could be swallowed by an animal in the ocean and survive, especially thousands of years before special effects and advanced technology. It seems impossible. But nothing is impossible with God!

Personally, I would doubt God's greatness if He wasn't powerful enough to perform miracles beyond our wildest imagination. But our God IS great! God's power and wisdom and compassion all run deeper than we can fathom.

Jonah not only survived being swallowed, but he lived inside the fish for three days until God commanded the fish and it vomited Jonah onto dry land. Scripture does not tell us what that smelled like or how it felt to be vomited out by a fish - though it was probably horribly disgusting. Instead, the Bible shows us a compassionate God who goes to great lengths to give salvation to everyone, not just the good kids.

Nineveh was an important city, but its people plotted against God and were cruel to innocent people. Yet God still wanted them to know and follow Him. So He sent Jonah to bring God's message of salvation to the city, but Jonah refused. Jonah ran and hid and even tried to sleep through God's commands. It wasn't until the great fish vomited him out that Jonah gave in and did what God asked.

Maybe you know someone at school or near your home like the people in Nineveh. You have seen them be mean to others. And now you do not even want to be around them. What would you do if God told you go talk to them, like He commanded Jonah to go speak to the people of Nineveh? What if you knew their salvation depended on you telling them about God? Would you go right away? Or would it take a miracle, like being swallowed and then vomited from a fish to make you obey?

God shows us through the book of Jonah that no one is beyond saving. No one is too bad to receive God's gift of salvation because God is compassionate and merciful. The Lord's heart is pure. God does not want anyone to die, not even an evil city, and He does not want His children to run away from what He calls us to do.

As you read God's story told through Jonah, think about how God is trying to change your story too. Who is He asking you to love that you think you can't? And when you think you can't, remember: God can!

READING PLAN

WEEK 1

GOD IS SOVEREIGN

Monday – God's will vs. my will
Read: Jonah 1:1-3, Psalm 139:7-10
SOAP: Psalm 139:7-10

Tuesday - God is always in control of the weather
Read: Jonah 1:4-6, Psalm 135:5-6
SOAP: Psalm 135:5-6

Wednesday - Stop running from God and obey
Read: Jonah 1:7-12, 1 John 2:4-6
SOAP: 1 John 2:4-6

Thursday – Admit your sin and move forward
Read: Jonah 1:13-17, 1 John 1:9
SOAP: 1 John 1:9

Friday – You can't hide from God
Read: Hebrews 4:12-13
SOAP: Hebrews 4:13

WEEK 2

GOD IS IN THE MIDST OF OUR STORMS...EVEN WHEN WE DISOBEY.

Monday - God can always hear our prayers
Read: Jonah 2:1-2, 1 John 5:14
SOAP: 1 John 5:14

Tuesday – God hears our cries for help
Read: Jonah 2:3-4, Psalm 31:22
SOAP: Psalm 31:22

Wednesday - God brings our lives out of the pit
Read: Jonah 2:5-7
SOAP: Jonah 2:6

Thursday - God responds to our gratitude
Read: Jonah 2:8-10, Psalm 50:23
SOAP: Psalm 50:23

Friday – God extends forgiveness and mercy
Read: Psalm 130:1-6
SOAP: Psalm 130:4-5

WEEK 3
POWER OF GOD'S MESSAGE

Monday - God is the giver of second chances
Read: Jonah 3:1-3, Lamentations 3:21-23
SOAP: Lamentations 3:21-23

Tuesday – God doesn't want anyone to perish
Read: Jonah 3:4-6, 2 Peter 3:9
SOAP: 2 Peter 3:9

Wednesday – God offers everlasting mercy
Read: Jonah 3:7-8, Proverbs 28:13
SOAP: Proverbs 28:13

Thursday - God is a God of compassion
Read: Jonah 3:9-10
SOAP: Jonah 3:10

Friday - God came into the world to save it, not condemn it
Read: John 3:17, Luke 19:10
SOAP: John 3:17

WEEK 4
GOD IS SLOW TO ANGER AND ABOUNDING IN STEADFAST LOVE

Monday – God is gracious to us
Read: Jonah 4:1-3
SOAP: Jonah 4:2

Tuesday - God holds the right to be angry, not us
Read: Jonah 4:4, Romans 3:23, Micah 6:8
SOAP: Romans 3:23, Micah 6:8

Wednesday - God is compassionate to us
Read: Jonah 4:5-9, Psalm 116:5, Psalm 103:10
SOAP: Psalm 116:5, Psalm 103:10

Thursday - God is more concerned about mercy than wrath
Read: Jonah 4:10-11, Romans 5:6-9
SOAP: Romans 5:6-9

Friday- God is good to all
Read: Psalm 145:8-9; Titus 2:11
SOAP: Psalm 145:8-9

YOUR GOALS

We believe it's important to write out goals for this study. Take some time now and write three goals you would like to focus on as you begin to rise each day and dig into God's Word. Make sure and refer back to these goals throughout the next weeks to help you stay focused. You can do it!

1.

2.

3.

Signature:

Date:

PRAYER

WRITE DOWN YOUR PRAYER REQUESTS AND PRAISES FOR EACH DAY.

Prayer focus for this week:
Spend time praying for your family members.

MONDAY

TUESDAY

WEDNESDAY

THURSDAY

FRIDAY

WEEK 1
God is Sovereign

Whatever the Lord pleases, he does, in heaven and on earth, in the seas and all deeps.

Psalm 135:6

_____

SCRIPTURE FOR WEEK 1

MONDAY

Jonah 1:1-3

1 Now the word of the Lord came to Jonah the son of Amittai, saying, 2 "Arise, go to Nineveh, that great city, and call out against it, for their evil has come up before me." 3 But Jonah rose to flee to Tarshish from the presence of the Lord. He went down to Joppa and found a ship going to Tarshish. So he paid the fare and went down into it, to go with them to Tarshish, away from the presence of the Lord.

Psalm 139:7-10

7 Where shall I go from your Spirit?
   Or where shall I flee from your presence?
8 If I ascend to heaven, you are there!
   If I make my bed in Sheol, you are there!
9 If I take the wings of the morning
   and dwell in the uttermost parts of the sea,
10 even there your hand shall lead me,
   and your right hand shall hold me.

TUESDAY

Jonah 1:4-6

4 But the Lord hurled a great wind upon the sea, and there was a mighty tempest on the sea, so that the ship threatened to break up. 5 Then the mariners were afraid, and each cried out to his god. And they hurled the cargo that was in the ship into the sea to lighten it for them. But Jonah had gone down into the inner part of the ship and had lain down and was fast asleep. 6 So the captain came and said to him, "What do you mean, you sleeper? Arise, call out to your god! Perhaps the god will give a thought to us, that we may not perish."

Psalm 135:5-6

5 For I know that the Lord is great,
   and that our Lord is above all gods.
6 Whatever the Lord pleases, he does,
   in heaven and on earth,
   in the seas and all deeps.

WEDNESDAY

Jonah 1:7-12

7 And they said to one another, "Come, let us cast lots, that we may know on whose account this evil has come upon us." So they cast lots, and the lot fell on Jonah. 8 Then they said to him, "Tell us on whose account this evil has come upon us. What is your occupation? And where do you come from? What is your country? And of what people are you?" 9 And he said to them, "I am a Hebrew, and I fear the Lord, the God of heaven, who made the sea and the dry land." 10 Then the men were exceedingly afraid and said to him, "What is this that you have done!" For the men knew that he was fleeing from the presence of the Lord, because he had told them.

11 Then they said to him, "What shall we do to you, that the sea may quiet down for us?" For the sea grew more and more tempestuous. 12 He said to them, "Pick me up and hurl me into the sea; then the sea will quiet down for you, for I know it is because of me that this great tempest has come upon you."

1 John 2:4-6

4 Whoever says "I know him" but does not keep his commandments is a liar, and the truth is not in him, 5 but whoever keeps his word, in him truly the love of God is perfected. By this we may know that we are in him: 6 whoever says he abides in him ought to walk in the same way in which he walked.

THURSDAY

Jonah 1:13-17

13 Nevertheless, the men rowed hard to get back to dry land, but they could not, for the sea grew more and more tempestuous against them. 14 Therefore they called out to the Lord, "O Lord, let us not perish for this man's life, and lay not on us innocent blood, for you, O Lord, have done as it pleased you." 15 So they picked up Jonah and hurled him into the sea, and the sea ceased from its raging. 16 Then the men feared the Lord exceedingly, and they offered a sacrifice to the Lord and made vows.

17 And the Lord appointed a great fish to swallow up Jonah. And Jonah was in the belly of the fish three days and three nights.

1 John 1:9

9 If we confess our sins, he is faithful and just to forgive us our sins and to cleanse us from all unrighteousness.

FRIDAY

Hebrews 4:12-13

12 For the word of God is living and active, sharper than any two-edged sword, piercing to the division of soul and of spirit, of joints and of marrow, and discerning the thoughts and intentions of the heart. 13 And no creature is hidden from his sight, but all are naked and exposed to the eyes of him to whom we must give account.

MONDAY

Read:
Jonah 1:1-3, Psalm 139:7-10
SOAP:
Psalm 139:7-10

1. Write out today's **SCRIPTURE** passage.

_____

_____

_____

_____

_____

_____

_____

_____

_____

2. On the blank page to the right, **DRAW** or **WRITE** what this passage means to you.

3. My **PRAYER** for today:

_____

_____

_____

_____

_____

TUESDAY

Read:
Jonah 1:4-6, Psalm 135:5-6
SOAP:
Psalm 135:5-6

1. Write out today's **SCRIPTURE** passage.

_____

_____

_____

_____

_____

_____

_____

_____

_____

_____

_____

2. On the blank page to the right, **DRAW** or **WRITE** what this passage means to you.

3. My **PRAYER** for today:

_____

_____

_____

_____

_____

WEDNESDAY

Read:
Jonah 1:7-12, 1 John 2:4-6
SOAP:
1 John 2:4-6

1. Write out today's **SCRIPTURE** passage.

_____

_____

_____

_____

_____

_____

_____

_____

_____

_____

2. On the blank page to the right, **DRAW** or **WRITE** what this passage means to you.

3. My **PRAYER** for today:

_____

_____

_____

_____

_____

THURSDAY

Read:
Jonah 1:13-17, 1 John 1:9

SOAP:
1 John 1:9

1. Write out today's **SCRIPTURE** passage.

_____

_____

_____

_____

_____

_____

_____

_____

_____

_____

2. On the blank page to the right, **DRAW** or **WRITE** what this passage means to you.

3. My **PRAYER** for today:

_____

_____

_____

_____

_____

FRIDAY

Read:
Hebrews 4:12-13

SOAP:
Hebrews 4:13

1. Write out today's **SCRIPTURE** passage.

_____

_____

_____

_____

_____

_____

_____

_____

_____

_____

2. On the blank page to the right, **DRAW** or **WRITE** what this passage means to you.

3. My **PRAYER** for today:

_____

_____

_____

_____

_____

THIS WEEK I LEARNED...

USE THE SPACE BELOW TO DRAW A PICTURE OR WRITE ABOUT WHAT YOU LEARNED THIS WEEK FROM YOUR TIME IN GOD'S WORD.

PRAYER

WRITE DOWN YOUR PRAYER REQUESTS AND PRAISES FOR EACH DAY.

Prayer focus for this week:
Spend time praying for your country.

MONDAY

TUESDAY

WEDNESDAY

THURSDAY

FRIDAY

WEEK 2

God is in the midst of our storms...
even when we disobey.

When my life was
fainting away, I
remembered the LORD,
and my prayer came
to you, into your holy
temple.

Jonah 2:7

_____

SCRIPTURE FOR WEEK 2

MONDAY

Jonah 2:1-2

1 Then Jonah prayed to the Lord his God from the belly of the fish, 2 saying,
"I called out to the Lord, out of my distress,
   and he answered me;
out of the belly of Sheol I cried,
   and you heard my voice.

1 John 5:14

14 And this is the confidence that we have toward him, that if we ask anything according to his will he hears us.

TUESDAY

Jonah 2:3-4

3 For you cast me into the deep,
   into the heart of the seas,
   and the flood surrounded me;
all your waves and your billows
   passed over me.
4 Then I said, 'I am driven away
   from your sight;
yet I shall again look
   upon your holy temple.'

Psalm 31:22

22 I had said in my alarm,
   "I am cut off from your sight."
But you heard the voice of my pleas for mercy
   when I cried to you for help.

WEDNESDAY

Jonah 2:5-7

5 The waters closed in over me to take my life;
   the deep surrounded me;

weeds were wrapped about my head
6 at the roots of the mountains.
I went down to the land
   whose bars closed upon me forever;
yet you brought up my life from the pit,
   O Lord my God.
7 When my life was fainting away,
   I remembered the Lord,
and my prayer came to you,
   into your holy temple.

THURSDAY

Jonah 2:8-10

8 Those who pay regard to vain idols
   forsake their hope of steadfast love.
9 But I with the voice of thanksgiving
   will sacrifice to you;
what I have vowed I will pay.
   Salvation belongs to the Lord!"
10 And the Lord spoke to the fish, and it vomited Jonah out upon the dry land.

Psalm 50:23

23 The one who offers thanksgiving as his sacrifice glorifies me;
   to one who orders his way rightly
   I will show the salvation of God!"

FRIDAY

Psalm 130:1-6

1 Out of the depths I cry to you, O Lord!
2 O Lord, hear my voice!
Let your ears be attentive
   to the voice of my pleas for mercy!
3 If you, O Lord, should mark iniquities,
   O Lord, who could stand?
4 But with you there is forgiveness,
   that you may be feared.
5 I wait for the Lord, my soul waits,
   and in his word I hope;
6 my soul waits for the Lord
   more than watchmen for the morning,
   more than watchmen for the morning.

MONDAY

Jonah 2:1-2, 1 John 5:14
SOAP:
1 John 5:14

1. Write out today's SCRIPTURE passage.

_____

_____

_____

_____

_____

_____

_____

_____

_____

_____

2. On the blank page to the right, DRAW or WRITE what this passage means to you.

3. My PRAYER for today:

_____

_____

_____

_____

_____

TUESDAY

Read:
Jonah 2:3-4, Psalm 31:22

SOAP:
Psalm 31:22

1. Write out today's **SCRIPTURE** passage.

_____

_____

_____

_____

_____

_____

_____

_____

_____

_____

2. On the blank page to the right, **DRAW** or **WRITE** what this passage means to you.

3. My **PRAYER** for today:

_____

_____

_____

_____

_____

WEDNESDAY

Read:
Jonah 2:5-7

SOAP:
Jonah 2:6

1. Write out today's SCRIPTURE passage.

_____

_____

_____

_____

_____

_____

_____

_____

_____

_____

2. On the blank page to the right, DRAW or WRITE what this passage means to you.

3. My PRAYER for today:

_____

_____

_____

_____

_____

THURSDAY

Read:
Jonah 2:8-10, Psalm 50:23

SOAP:
Psalm 50:23

1. Write out today's **SCRIPTURE** passage.

_____

_____

_____

_____

_____

_____

_____

_____

_____

_____

2. On the blank page to the right, **DRAW** or **WRITE** what this passage means to you.

3. My **PRAYER** for today:

_____

_____

_____

_____

_____

FRIDAY

Read:
Psalm 130:1-6

SOAP:
Psalm 130:4-5

1. Write out today's **SCRIPTURE** passage.

_____

_____

_____

_____

_____

_____

_____

_____

_____

_____

2. On the blank page to the right, **DRAW** or **WRITE** what this passage means to you.

3. My **PRAYER** for today:

_____

_____

_____

_____

_____

THIS WEEK I LEARNED...

USE THE SPACE BELOW TO DRAW A PICTURE OR WRITE ABOUT WHAT YOU LEARNED THIS WEEK FROM YOUR TIME IN GOD'S WORD.

PRAYER

WRITE DOWN YOUR PRAYER REQUESTS AND PRAISES FOR EACH DAY.

Prayer focus for this week:
Spend time praying for your friends.

MONDAY

TUESDAY

WEDNESDAY

THURSDAY

FRIDAY

WEEK 3
Power of God's Message

Whoever conceals his transgressions will not prosper, but he who confesses and forsakes them will obtain mercy.

Proverbs 28:13

SCRIPTURE FOR WEEK 3

MONDAY

Jonah 3:1-3

1 Then the word of the Lord came to Jonah the second time, saying, 2 "Arise, go to Nineveh, that great city, and call out against it the message that I tell you." 3 So Jonah arose and went to Nineveh, according to the word of the Lord. Now Nineveh was an exceedingly great city, three days' journey in breadth.

Lamentations 3:21-23

21 But this I call to mind,
   and therefore I have hope:
22 The steadfast love of the Lord never ceases;
   his mercies never come to an end;
23 they are new every morning;
   great is your faithfulness.

TUESDAY

Jonah 3:4-6

4 Jonah began to go into the city, going a day's journey. And he called out, "Yet forty days, and Nineveh shall be overthrown!" 5 And the people of Nineveh believed God. They called for a fast and put on sackcloth, from the greatest of them to the least of them.

6 The word reached the king of Nineveh, and he arose from his throne, removed his robe, covered himself with sackcloth, and sat in ashes.

2 Peter 3:9

9 The Lord is not slow to fulfill his promise as some count slowness, but is patient toward you, not wishing that any should perish, but that all should reach repentance.

WEDNESDAY

Jonah 3:7-8

7 And he issued a proclamation and published through Nineveh, "By the decree of the king and his nobles: Let neither man nor beast, herd nor flock, taste anything. Let them not feed

or drink water, 8 but let man and beast be covered with sackcloth, and let them call out mightily to God. Let everyone turn from his evil way and from the violence that is in his hands.

Proverbs 28:13

13 Whoever conceals his transgressions will not prosper,
   but he who confesses and forsakes them will obtain mercy.

THURSDAY

Jonah 3:9-10

9 Who knows? God may turn and relent and turn from his fierce anger, so that we may not perish."

10 When God saw what they did, how they turned from their evil way, God relented of the disaster that he had said he would do to them, and he did not do it.

FRIDAY

John 3:17

17 For God did not send his Son into the world to condemn the world, but in order that the world might be saved through him.

Luke 19:10

10 For the Son of Man came to seek and to save the lost."

MONDAY

Read:
Jonah 3:1-3, Lamentations 3:21-23
SOAP:
Lamentations 3:21-23

1. Write out today's **SCRIPTURE** passage.

_____

_____

_____

_____

_____

_____

_____

_____

_____

_____

2. On the blank page to the right, **DRAW** or **WRITE** what this passage means to you.

3. My **PRAYER** for today:

_____

_____

_____

_____

_____

TUESDAY

Jonah 3:4-6, 2 Peter 3:9

SOAP:
2 Peter 3:9

1. Write out today's **SCRIPTURE** passage.

_____

_____

_____

_____

_____

_____

_____

_____

_____

_____

2. On the blank page to the right, **DRAW** or **WRITE** what this passage means to you.

3. My **PRAYER** for today:

_____

_____

_____

_____

_____

WEDNESDAY

Read:
Jonah 3:7-8, Proverbs 28:13

SOAP:
Proverbs 28:13

1. Write out today's **SCRIPTURE** passage.

_____

_____

_____

_____

_____

_____

_____

_____

_____

_____

2. On the blank page to the right, **DRAW** or **WRITE** what this passage means to you.

3. My **PRAYER** for today:

_____

_____

_____

_____

_____

THURSDAY

Jonah 3:9-10

SOAP:
Jonah 3:10

1. Write out today's **SCRIPTURE** passage.

_____

_____

_____

_____

_____

_____

_____

_____

_____

_____

2. On the blank page to the right, **DRAW** or **WRITE** what this passage means to you.

3. My **PRAYER** for today:

_____

_____

_____

_____

_____

_____

FRIDAY

Read:
John 3:17, Luke 19:10

SOAP:
John 3:17

1. Write out today's **SCRIPTURE** passage.

_____

_____

_____

_____

_____

_____

_____

_____

_____

_____

2. On the blank page to the right, **DRAW** or **WRITE** what this passage means to you.

3. My **PRAYER** for today:

_____

_____

_____

_____

_____

THIS WEEK I LEARNED...

USE THE SPACE BELOW TO DRAW A PICTURE OR WRITE ABOUT WHAT YOU LEARNED THIS WEEK FROM YOUR TIME IN GOD'S WORD.

PRAYER

WRITE DOWN YOUR PRAYER REQUESTS AND PRAISES FOR EACH DAY.

Prayer focus for this week:
Spend time praying for your church.

MONDAY

TUESDAY

WEDNESDAY

THURSDAY

FRIDAY

WEEK 4

God is slow to anger and abounding in steadfast love

The LORD is gracious and merciful, slow to anger and abounding in steadfast love.

Psalm 145:8

_____

SCRIPTURE FOR WEEK 4

MONDAY

Jonah 4:1-3

1 But it displeased Jonah exceedingly, and he was angry. 2 And he prayed to the Lord and said, "O Lord, is not this what I said when I was yet in my country? That is why I made haste to flee to Tarshish; for I knew that you are a gracious God and merciful, slow to anger and abounding in steadfast love, and relenting from disaster. 3 Therefore now, O Lord, please take my life from me, for it is better for me to die than to live."

TUESDAY

Jonah 4:4

4 And the Lord said, "Do you do well to be angry?"

Romans 3:23

23 for all have sinned and fall short of the glory of God,

Micah 6:8

8 He has told you, O man, what is good;
   and what does the Lord require of you
but to do justice, and to love kindness,
   and to walk humbly with your God?

WEDNESDAY

Jonah 4:5-9

5 Jonah went out of the city and sat to the east of the city and made a booth for himself there. He sat under it in the shade, till he should see what would become of the city. 6 Now the Lord God appointed a plant and made it come up over Jonah, that it might be a shade over his head, to save him from his discomfort. So Jonah was exceedingly glad because of the plant. 7 But when dawn came up the next day, God appointed a worm that attacked the plant, so that it withered. 8 When the sun rose, God appointed a scorching east wind, and the sun beat down on the head of Jonah so that he was faint. And he asked that he might die and said, "It is better for me to die than to live." 9 But God said to Jonah, "Do you do well to be angry for the plant?" And he said, "Yes, I do well to be angry, angry enough to die."

Psalm 116:5

5 Gracious is the Lord, and righteous;
  our God is merciful.

Psalm 103:10

10 He does not deal with us according to our sins,
  nor repay us according to our iniquities.

THURSDAY

Jonah 4:10-11

10 And the Lord said, "You pity the plant, for which you did not labor, nor did you make it grow, which came into being in a night and perished in a night. 11 And should not I pity Nineveh, that great city, in which there are more than 120,000 persons who do not know their right hand from their left, and also much cattle?"

Romans 5:6-9

6 For while we were still weak, at the right time Christ died for the ungodly. 7 For one will scarcely die for a righteous person—though perhaps for a good person one would dare even to die— 8 but God shows his love for us in that while we were still sinners, Christ died for us. 9 Since, therefore, we have now been justified by his blood, much more shall we be saved by him from the wrath of God.

FRIDAY

Psalm 145:8-9

8 The Lord is gracious and merciful,
  slow to anger and abounding in steadfast love.
9 The Lord is good to all,
  and his mercy is over all that he has made.

Titus 2:11

11 For the grace of God has appeared, bringing salvation for all people,

MONDAY

Read:
Jonah 4:1-3

SOAP:
Jonah 4:2

1. Write out today's **SCRIPTURE** passage.

_____

_____

_____

_____

_____

_____

_____

_____

_____

_____

2. On the blank page to the right, **DRAW** or **WRITE** what this passage means to you.

3. My **PRAYER** for today:

_____

_____

_____

_____

_____

_____

TUESDAY

Read:
Jonah 4:4, Romans 3:23, Micah 6:8

SOAP:
Romans 3:23, Micah 6:8

1. Write out today's **SCRIPTURE** passage.

_____

_____

_____

_____

_____

_____

_____

_____

_____

_____

2. On the blank page to the right, **DRAW** or **WRITE** what this passage means to you.

3. My **PRAYER** for today:

_____

_____

_____

_____

_____

WEDNESDAY

Read:
Jonah 4:5-9, Psalm 116:5, Psalm 103:10
SOAP:
Psalm 116:5, Psalm 103:10

1. Write out today's **SCRIPTURE** passage.

_____

_____

_____

_____

_____

_____

_____

_____

_____

_____

2. On the blank page to the right, **DRAW** or **WRITE** what this passage means to you.

3. My **PRAYER** for today:

_____

_____

_____

_____

_____

_____

THURSDAY

Read:
Jonah 4:10-11, Romans 5:6-9

SOAP:
Romans 5:6-9

1. Write out today's **SCRIPTURE** passage.

_____

_____

_____

_____

_____

_____

_____

_____

_____

_____

2. On the blank page to the right, **DRAW** or **WRITE** what this passage means to you.

3. My **PRAYER** for today:

_____

_____

_____

_____

_____

_____

FRIDAY

Read:
Psalm 145:8-9; Titus 2:11

SOAP:
Psalm 145:8-9

1. Write out today's **SCRIPTURE** passage.

_____

_____

_____

_____

_____

_____

_____

_____

_____

_____

2. On the blank page to the right, **DRAW** or **WRITE** what this passage means to you.

3. My **PRAYER** for today:

_____

_____

_____

_____

_____

_____

THIS WEEK I LEARNED...

USE THE SPACE BELOW TO DRAW A PICTURE OR WRITE ABOUT WHAT YOU LEARNED THIS WEEK FROM YOUR TIME IN GOD'S WORD.

Made in the USA
Middletown, DE
20 August 2018